Heinemann First
ENCYCLOPEDIA

Volume 8
Mou-Pen

Heinemann Library
Chicago, Illinois

Series Editors: Rebecca and Stephen Vickers, Gianna Williams
Author Team: Rob Alcraft, Catherine Chambers, Sabrina Crewe, Jim Drake, Fred Martin, Angela Royston, Jane Shuter, Roger Thomas, Rebecca Vickers, Stephen Vickers

This revised and expanded edition produced for Heinemann Library by Discovery Books.
Photo research by Katherine Smith and Rachel Tisdale
Designed by Keith Williams, Michelle Lisseter, and Gecko
Illustrations by Stefan Chabluk and Mark Bergin

Originated by Ambassador Litho Limited
Printed in China by WKT Company Limited

10 09 08 07 06
10 9 8 7 6 5 4 3 2

Library of Congress Cataloging-in-Publication Data

Heinemann first encyclopedia.
    p. cm.
  Summary: A fourteen-volume encyclopedia covering animals, plants, countries, transportation, science, ancient civilizations, US states, US presidents, and world history
    ISBN 1-4034-7115-0 (v. 8 : lib. bdg.)
   1. Children's encyclopedias and dictionaries.
I. Heinemann Library (Firm)
AG5.H45 2005
031—dc22
                                        2005006176

Acknowledgments

Cover: Cover photographs of a desert, an electric guitar, a speedboat, an iceberg, a man on a camel, cactus flowers, and the Colosseum at night reproduced with permission of Corbis. Cover photograph of the Taj Mahal reproduced with permission of Digital Stock. Cover photograph of an x-ray of a man reproduced with permission of Digital Vision. Cover photographs of a giraffe, the Leaning Tower of Pisa, the Statue of Liberty, a white owl, a cactus, a butterfly, a saxophone, an astronaut, cars at night, and a circuit board reproduced with permission of Getty Images/Photodisc. Cover photograph of Raglan Castle reproduced with permission of Peter Evans; C. Borland/PhotoLink, p. 10; J. Allan Cash Ltd., pp. 11, 12, 18, 19, 20, 24, 25, 26, 34 bottom, 42 bottom, 43, 44, 46; Ancient Art and Architecture, p. 33; BBC Music Live/Henrietta Butler, p. 36; Bridgeman Art Library, p. 42 top; Willard Clay/Taxi, p. 23; Corbis-Bettman, p. 8; Michael Leach, p. 5 bottom; Survival Anglia/Danial Vall p. 4; Redferns, p. 6; Empics, p. 27; D. Falconer/PhotoLink, p. 16; Kent Knudson/PhotoLink, p. 31; Oxford Scientific Films, p. 29; Doug Allen, p. 48 bottom; Tony Bomford, p. 41 top; Stanley Breeden, p. 47 bottom; Neil Bromaic, p. 35 bottom; Daniel Cox, p. 40 bottom; Tim Davies, p. 38; Rudie Kuper, p. 30 bottom; Dr. Richard K. La Val, p. 47 top; Lon Lauber, p. 39 bottom; Kjell Sandved, pp. 45 bottom, 48 top; F. Schussler/PhotoLink, p. 32; Keren Su, p. 45 top; Tom Ulrich, p. 35 top; Norbert Wu, p. 30 top; Performing Arts Library, p. 34 top; RSPCA Photo Library/John George, p. 39 top; Scenics of America/PhotoLink, pp. 13, 15, 17, 37; S. Solum/PhotoLink, pp. 14, 22; Still Pictures/Michael Gunther, p. 21; Trip/H. Rogers, p. 41 bottom.

Every effort has been made to contact copyright holders of any material reproduced in this book. Any omissions will be rectified in subsequent printings if notice is given to the Publisher.

Welcome to
Heinemann First Encyclopedia

What is an encyclopedia?

An encyclopedia is an information book. It gives the most important facts about many different subjects. This encyclopedia has been written for children who are using an encyclopedia for the first time. It covers many of the subjects from school and others you may find interesting.

What is in this encyclopedia?

In this encyclopedia, each topic is called an *entry*. There is one page of information for every entry. The entries in this encyclopedia explain

- animals
- plants
- dinosaurs
- countries
- geography
- history
- world religions
- music
- art
- transportation
- science
- technology
- states
- famous Americans

How to use this encyclopedia

This encyclopedia has thirteen books called *volumes*. The first twelve volumes contain entries. The entries are all in alphabetical order. This means that Volume 1 starts with entries that begin with the letter A and Volume 12 ends with entries that begin with the letter Z. Volume 13 is the index volume. It also has other interesting information.

Here are two entries that show you what you can find on a page:

This is the letter that the entry starts with.

Fact boxes give you details about the topic.

The "see also" line tells you where to find other related information.

Did You Know? boxes have fun or interesting bits of information.

The Fact File tells you important facts and figures.

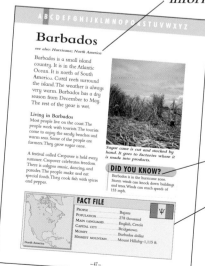

Mountain

see also: Island, Volcano

Mountains are areas of high land. The land has steep, sloping sides. The highest point on a mountain is called the peak. A mountain is usually over 1,600 feet high. Most mountains are part of a large group. The group is called a mountain range or a chain.

How mountains are made

Mountains are usually made when flat layers of rock are pushed by forces in the earth. The layers can be pushed so much that they make giant ripples. The ripples are called folds. Some mountains are volcanoes. Molten rock flows out of them. They grow bigger every time they erupt. Some mountains rise from the ocean floor. Their peaks make small islands.

DID YOU KNOW?

The 25 highest mountains in the world are all in the Himalayan and Karakoram mountain ranges. These two ranges are in the same area of Asia. These mountains are still getting bigger.

People and mountains

Not many people live in high mountains. The land can be too steep. The climate can be too cold and wet to grow crops. People can enjoy mountain sports, such as skiing and climbing. Mountains are good places to build reservoirs to store water. Water flows quickly down mountains. It can be used to make electricity in power plants.

Mountains are used for winter sports such as skiing and snowboarding.

Mouse

see also: Mammal

A mouse is a very small mammal. It is about as big as a chicken egg. A mouse is covered in fur. It has a long, thin tail. The word "mice" is used for more than one mouse. Mice have large front teeth for nibbling. They eat nuts and fruit.

Mouse families

A male mouse is called a buck. A female mouse is called a doe. Mouse babies are called cubs. Cubs are born blind, deaf, and hairless. Their eyes open after one week. A doe can give birth to a hundred cubs in one year.

tail to balance when running and climbing

MOUSE FACTS

NUMBER OF KINDS	1,082 mice and rats
COLOR	brown, black, white, gray
LENGTH	about 3 inches with a tail the same length
STATUS	common
LIFE SPAN	about 2 years
ENEMIES	cats, birds of prey, people

ears for good hearing

eyes on the sides of the head for all-around vision

claws for gripping

a harvest mouse

PLANT, INSECT, AND MEAT EATER

Wild mice have lived with humans for about 10 thousand years. Houses and farm buildings are warm places to live. There is plenty of food, such as grain. Mice also eat insects and household scraps.

This is a nest of wood mice cubs. They will soon look like their mother.

Music

*see also: Classical Music, Jazz, Musical
Instrument, Percussion Instrument,
Stringed Instrument, Wind Instrument*

Music is making sounds using
voices and instruments. Human
beings have sung and chanted
from earliest times. No one knows
what very early music was like.

Music around the world

There are many different kinds of music.
Each part of the world has its own
special kind of music. Flamenco music
is from Spain. Gamelan music is from
Indonesia. Today many types of music
are made and enjoyed all over the
world. Today's music includes pop music,
classical music, folk, and jazz.

*This musician from India is playing
a stringed instrument. It is called a
sitar. India's musical tradition is
hundreds of years old.*

*The famous jazz musician Dizzy
Gillespie played his specially-made
trumpet. The trumpet is also played
in popular and classical music.*

PYTHAGORAS (582–500 B.C.)

The ancient Greek philosopher,
Pythagoras, had some of the earliest
ideas about music. He discovered that
mathematics could be applied to musical
notes. This idea led to the way a lot of
music is composed and written.

Musical Instrument

see also: Music, Percussion Instrument, Stringed Instrument, Wind Instrument

Musical instruments are made for making music. They can be as simple as a triangle. They can also be as complicated as an electronic keyboard. Everyday objects, like spoons or dried seed pods, can also be musical instruments.

JIMI HENDRIX (1942–1970)

Jimi Hendrix was an American musician. He played the electric guitar. Hendrix was always looking for new ways to make sounds. In one of his songs, he hummed through a comb covered in paper.

This Aboriginal Australian musician is using a stick to beat out a rhythm.

Jimi Hendrix played the electric guitar. The electric guitar is a very popular modern instrument.

The first instruments

People began by using parts of their bodies to make sounds. They clapped their hands, stamped their feet, and listened to the rhythm of their heartbeats. The first instruments were sticks beating out rhythms.

Instruments today

Today instruments are grouped by the way they make sounds. Some instruments use strings. Some use the musician's breath. Some are hit or shaken. Some make electronic sounds.

Myth

see also: Legend, Literature, Story

Myths are stories about gods, goddesses, and spirits. Myths often try to explain how the world was created. Myths also try to explain how important discoveries, such as fire, were made.

Greek, Roman, and Norse myths

The most famous myths are the myths of the ancient Greeks and Romans, and the Norse myths of the Vikings. These myths tell how the ancient people saw the world. Many myths tell how the gods and goddesses came to Earth and played tricks on or fell in love with human beings.

Myths said that things like thunder and lightning were signs of the gods' anger.

This Native American drum is painted with a mythical bird.

Myths of native people

The Native Americans, the Aborigines in Australia, and the Maoris in New Zealand also have many myths. The myths of different tribes explain how things happened in the world. Most Native American myths are about animals that represent the spirits of the earth.

Native Americans

see also: North America, Sacagawea

Native Americans were the first people of North America. They have lived in North America for about 15–30 thousand years. Today there are more than 4 million Native Americans in North America.

Land and life

Native Americans are divided into groups called tribes. The Mohawk tribe lived in the northeast. They lived in homes called longhouses. Many families shared the same longhouse. They grew corn and hunted deer.

Some of the Native Americans lived in forests. They used rivers as their roads.

Tribes such as the Lakota lived on the grassy plains. They lived in teepees. They hunted bison. Their teepees could be taken apart and moved. Then the Lakota could follow the herds of bison.

Native Americans today

Most tribes had their land taken from them when European settlers arrived. Many Native Americans were moved to special areas called reservations. Many tribes have kept their traditions alive.

When tribes moved, they carried their belongings on a travois.

Nebraska

see also: United States of America

Nebraska is a state in the central United States of America. It is on the Great Plains. The land is mostly flat grassland. There are hills in the northern part of the state. The weather is quite dry. Summers are hot and winters are cold.

In the past

Long ago, the Plains Indians lived on the plains of Nebraska. They hunted bison and gathered wild plants for food. Later, homesteaders came and settled in Nebraska. They dug wells to reach underground water. They built farms.

DID YOU KNOW?

Most states have two legislative houses. Nebraska is the only state that has just one. It is called the Nebraska Unicameral Legislature.

Covered wagons sit under Eagle Rock, Nebraska.

Life in Nebraska

Today, farmers in Nebraska produce huge amounts of wheat, corn, and sorghum. They raise cattle and hogs, too. Manufacturing is also important in Nebraska. Workers in factories process crops and meat raised in the state. Some factories make machinery and electrical equipment.

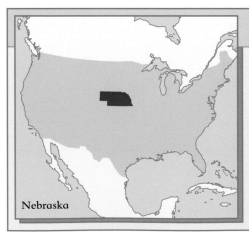

Nebraska

FACT FILE

BECAME A STATE...	1867 (37th state)
LAND AREA.........	76,872 square miles (15th largest land area)
POPULATION	1,739,291 (38th most populated state)
OTHER NAME	Cornhusker State
CAPITAL CITY	Lincoln

Nepal

see also: Asia, Mountain

Nepal is in Asia. It is a small country. It is one of the world's highest countries. Most of Nepal is in the Himalaya Mountains. Almost half of Nepal is covered with forests. It is warmer and wetter lower down in the valleys.

Living in Nepal

Nearly everyone works on farms. Rice and vegetables are the most important crops. Some farmers raise goats, cattle, and buffalo. They also cut down trees to sell the wood. People from the Sherpa tribe often work as mountain guides for tourists and visiting climbers.

Most Nepalese are Hindus. They believe in many gods and goddesses. People often celebrate holy days by washing in a river or lake. They sing and dance to celebrate weddings and farming events.

This cart is part of the Nepalese New Year festival.

DID YOU KNOW?

A Nepalese Sherpa named Tenzing Norgay and the New Zealand mountain climber, Sir Edmund Hillary, were the first people to reach the top of Mount Everest in the Himalayas. They reached the top of the world's tallest mountain on May 29, 1953. They had climbed for two months.

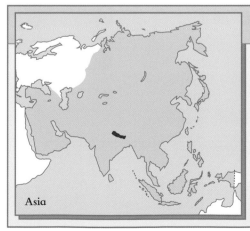

Asia

FACT FILE

PEOPLE	Nepalese
POPULATION	about 27 million
MAIN LANGUAGE	Nepali
CAPITAL CITY	Katmandu
MONEY	Nepalese rupee
HIGHEST MOUNTAIN	Mount Everest—29,028 feet
LONGEST RIVER	River Ghaghara—571 miles

Netherlands

see also: Europe

The Netherlands is a country in northwest Europe. It has a coast along the North Sea. Most of the land is low and flat. Some of the land used to be underwater. The people used pumps and walls called dikes to drain land. These land areas are called polders.

The Netherlands are famous for their tulips and windmills. The windmills used to pump water away from flooded land. Now most pumping is done by big machines.

Living in the Netherlands

Dutch farmers grow crops. They raise herds of dairy cows. Dutch cheese is sold in many countries. Some farmers grow tulips and other flowers. There are big factories in the ports of Rotterdam and Amsterdam.

Some of the world's most famous artists were Dutch. The painters Rembrandt, Van Gogh, and Vermeer were born in the Netherlands.

DID YOU KNOW?

People sometimes call this country Holland. One part of the Netherlands is called Holland, but this is not the correct name for the whole country.

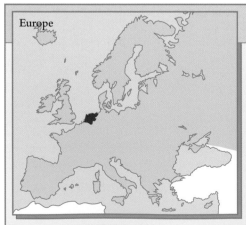

Europe

FACT FILE

PEOPLE	Dutch, Netherlanders
POPULATION	about 16 million
MAIN LANGUAGES	Dutch
CAPITAL CITY	Amsterdam
MONEY	Euro
HIGHEST LAND	Vaalserberg—1,054 feet
LONGEST RIVER	River Rhine—820 miles

Nevada

see also: United States of America

Nevada is a state in the western United States of America. It has mountains and desert. There are high plateaus and deep canyons. The weather is very hot in Nevada in summer. It is the driest of all the 50 states because it receives the least rainfall.

In the past

Many people came to Nevada in the 1800s to mine for gold and silver. Mining is still an important industry there. Nevada produces 40 percent of the nation's silver. Gold is the state's most valuable mineral.

DID YOU KNOW?

There are hundreds of ghost towns in Nevada. They were once busy places where miners lived. Now the buildings are empty.

Las Vegas is world-famous for its bright lights and nightlife.

Life in Nevada

Las Vegas is Nevada's largest city, with a population of about half a million people. In Nevada, tourism provides more jobs than any other industry. People work in hotels, restaurants, and casinos. They work at lakes where visitors come to swim and water-ski.

Nevada

FACT FILE

BECAME A STATE... 1864 (36th state)

LAND AREA......... 109,826 square miles
(7th largest land area)

POPULATION 2,241,154
(35th most populated state)

OTHER NAMES ..... Sagebrush State, Silver State, Battle Born State

CAPITAL CITY ...... Carson City

New Hampshire

see also: United States of America

New Hampshire is a state in the northeastern United States of America. There are many hills and mountains. New Hampshire has a stretch of coast in the south of the state. Near the coast, the weather can be mild. In the mountains to the north, there is lots of snow.

There are many historic buildings in New Hampshire, like this church and bridge.

In the past

New Hampshire has many lakes and rivers. In the 1800s, people used the water to power mills and factories.

DID YOU KNOW?

New Hampshire was the first British colony to declare independence from Britain. It adopted its own constitution in January 1776. A few months later, New Hampshire's delegates cast the first vote in favor of the Declaration of Independence.

Life in New Hampshire

Today, manufacturing is the most important industry in New Hampshire. People work in factories making computers and other electronic equipment. They also produce plastic, metal, and paper products. Farmers in the state produce dairy products. They raise chickens and grow hay, fruit, and vegetables. Craftspeople make traditional baskets, rugs, and pottery.

New Hampshire

FACT FILE

BECAME A STATE... 1788 (9th state)

LAND AREA......... 8,968 square miles
(44th largest land area)

POPULATION 1,287,687
(41st most populated state)

OTHER NAME ...... Granite State

CAPITAL CITY ...... Concord

New Jersey

see also: United States of America

New Jersey is a state in the eastern United States of America. There are mountains in the north. In the center of the state are high, rolling lands. The land is lower in the south and east. New Jersey has many beaches. The weather is warmer by the ocean. In the mountains, summers are cooler and winters are cold.

People stroll along the boardwalk in Atlantic City.

Life in New Jersey

New Jersey has a lot of people living in a small state. It is very crowded. Millions more people come as tourists every year. Resort towns line New Jersey's coast. Atlantic City is one of the world's largest seaside resorts. Lots of visitors come to visit casinos, hotels, and restaurants.

DID YOU KNOW?

In 1858, a fossilized hadrosaurus skeleton was discovered in Haddonfield, New Jersey. It was the first dinosaur skeleton ever found in the United States.

New Jersey is also a center for the chemical industry. It has many scientific research centers. The state's factories make shampoo, paint, and medicines. New Jersey's farmers grow flowers, vegetables, and fruit.

New Jersey

FACT FILE

BECAME A STATE... 1787 (3rd state)

LAND AREA......... 7,417 square miles
(46th largest land area)

POPULATION 8,638,396
(10th most populated state)

OTHER NAME ...... Garden State

CAPITAL CITY ...... Trenton

New Mexico

see also: United States of America

New Mexico is a state in the southwestern United States of America. There are mountains, deserts, and forests. New Mexico is very dry. It is warm in lower areas and gets colder in higher places.

Life in New Mexico

The Rio Grande is a river that runs all the way through western New Mexico. Its valley makes good farmland for chili peppers, cotton, and pecans. Cattle and sheep graze on the Great Plains in the east of the state.

Some people in New Mexico work in scientific fields, particularly energy and defense. Others mine the state's natural resources, such as uranium and oil. Factories make food products and machinery.

Many people in New Mexico come from Native American or Spanish

This is the Spanish mission at San Jose de Laguna, New Mexico.

DID YOU KNOW?

Santa Fe was founded in 1610. It is the oldest and highest capital city in the United States. Albuquerque is the largest city in New Mexico. Every year, it hosts the world's biggest hot air balloon festival.

cultures. The Navajo reservation covers millions of acres in New Mexico. Pueblo Indians live at Taos Pueblo. Their people have lived there for over 800 years.

New Mexico

FACT FILE

BECAME A STATE...	1912 (47th state)
LAND AREA.........	121,356 square miles
	(5th largest land area)
POPULATION	1,874,614
	(36th most populated state)
OTHER NAME	Land of Enchantment
CAPITAL CITY	Santa Fe

New York

see also: Statue of Liberty

New York is a state in the northeastern United States of America. There are mountains, hills, and forests in the north and east. There are beaches on Long Island in the southern part of the state. Other regions have low land good for farming. Some of New York has a mild climate. The north gets very cold in winter. There is lots of snow in the west.

Central Park is a vast expanse of green in the middle of New York City.

DID YOU KNOW?

Niagara Falls in western New York and Canada is the second largest waterfall in the world. The American Falls are on the U.S. side. The Horseshoe Falls are on the Canadian side.

Life in New York

New York City is the biggest city in the United States. It is the business center of the nation, too. About half the people in the state of New York live in the New York City area. New York has one of the world's busiest ports and airports. Millions of people come to New York City as tourists.

Elsewhere in the state, factories produce electronic equipment, instruments, and machinery. Workers grind flour and make toys. Farmers grow fruit and vegetables and raise cows for dairy produce.

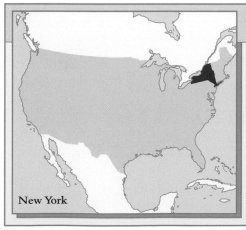

New York

FACT FILE

BECAME A STATE... 1788 (11th state)

LAND AREA......... 47,214 square miles
(30th largest land area)

POPULATION 19,190,115
(3rd most populated state)

OTHER NAME ...... Empire State

CAPITAL CITY...... Albany

New Zealand

see also: Australia and Oceania, Kiwi

New Zealand is a country in the south Pacific Ocean. It has two main islands. North Island has volcanoes, hot springs, and mountains. South Island has lakes, forests, glaciers, and mountains.

Living in New Zealand

Most New Zealanders live and work in the cities. Food products are made in factories. These products are sold to other countries. Farmers grow grains, potatoes, fruit, and vegetables. Sheep and cattle are raised on large farms.

Europeans settled in New Zealand. They are the ancestors of most of the people. The native people are called the Maori. Many places have Maori names. Two shellfish are used in Maori recipes. The fish are *toheroa* and *tuatua*.

These Maori women are dancing at a local festival.

DID YOU KNOW?

The national bird of New Zealand is the kiwi. It is a bird that cannot fly. New Zealanders are sometimes called "Kiwis."

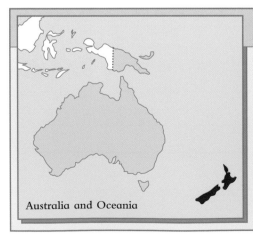

Australia and Oceania

FACT FILE

PEOPLE	New Zealanders
POPULATION	almost 4 million
MAIN LANGUAGES	English, Maori
CAPITAL CITY	Wellington
BIGGEST CITY	Auckland
MONEY	New Zealand dollar
HIGHEST MOUNTAIN	Mount Cook—12,317 feet
LONGEST RIVER	Waikato—270 miles

Nicaragua

see also: North America

Nicaragua is a small country in Central America. Nicaragua has mountains with volcanoes. The volcanoes still erupt. Earthquakes sometimes cause a lot of damage. There is flat land along the east coast. This coast is called Mosquito Coast. There are two very big lakes. There is wet rain forest and dry grassland.

DID YOU KNOW?

Native American people lived in Nicaragua before Spanish settlers arrived. The name Nicaragua comes from the name, *Nicarao.* Nicarao was a Native American chief.

Living in Nicaragua

Most people work on farms. They grow corn, beans, rice, coffee, and cotton. Cattle are raised on big ranches. There are mines for digging gold and copper.

Tourists visit the beaches and the lakes. The lakes are in the craters of inactive volcanoes. Nicaraguans enjoy dancing to lively marimba music. Their favorite foods are tortillas and fried rice with beans.

This is the main road through a Nicaraguan village.

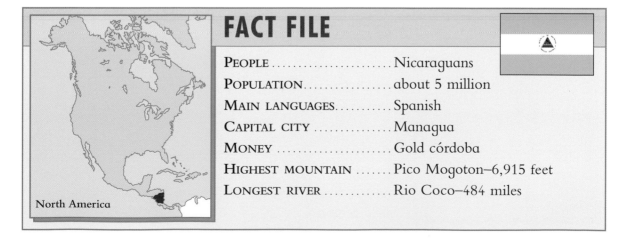

North America

FACT FILE

PEOPLE	Nicaraguans
POPULATION	about 5 million
MAIN LANGUAGES	Spanish
CAPITAL CITY	Managua
MONEY	Gold córdoba
HIGHEST MOUNTAIN	Pico Mogoton—6,915 feet
LONGEST RIVER	Rio Coco—484 miles

Pendleton Community Library

Nigeria

see also: Africa

Nigeria is a country in West Africa. The north is hot with grasslands. The south has rain forests. The east has mountains. The coast is swampy.

Living in Nigeria

More people live in Nigeria than in any other country in Africa. Most Nigerians live in the country. Farmers grow cocoa, grains, cotton, cassava, yams, and peanuts. Nigeria sells oil to other countries.

Nigeria has 250 different tribal groups. The groups have many languages and customs. Nigerians celebrate harvests with festivals. They sing special songs and do drumming. A favorite food is bean cakes. The cakes are fried in peanut oil. Then they are eaten with okra and spicy sauces.

People in rural areas grind grain with a large stick. The crushed grain is used to make food.

DID YOU KNOW?

Nigeria's capital city, Abuja, is a new city. It was finished in 1991. Today more than one million people live there.

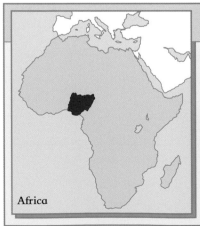

Africa

FACT FILE

PEOPLE	Nigerians
POPULATION	about 137 million
MAIN LANGUAGES	English, Hausa, Yoruba, Ibo
CAPITAL CITY	Abuja
BIGGEST CITY	Lagos
MONEY	Naira
HIGHEST MOUNTAIN	Dimlang—6,702 feet
LONGEST RIVER	Niger-Benue—2,590 miles

North America

see also: Continent, Native Americans

North America is the third largest continent. There are eighteen countries in North America. The Atlantic Ocean is to the east. The Pacific Ocean is to the west. Most of North America is flat, grassy land. This land is called plains. The Rocky Mountains are in the west.

Climate, plants, and animals

The coldest places are in the far north. It is hot in the south near the Gulf of Mexico and the Caribbean Sea. There are deserts, rain forests, and grasslands in Mexico and Central America. Bears and wolves live in the large pine forests in the north.

People in North America

The first people to live in North America were the Native Americans. Over time, people from many other countries have come to live in North America. About 481 million people now live in North America.

DID YOU KNOW?

Death Valley is in the United States. It is one of the hottest places in the world. The temperature is sometimes higher than 125°F.

NORTH AMERICA FACTS

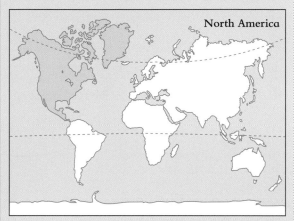

North America

SIZE	about 9 million square miles
LARGEST CITY	Mexico City
HIGHEST MOUNTAIN	Mount McKinley—20,320 feet
LONGEST RIVER	Mississippi—Missouri— Red Rock Rivers—3,877 miles
SPECIAL FEATURES	the five Great Lakes, Niagara Falls

Niagara Falls are on the border between the United States and Canada.

North Carolina

see also: United States of America

North Carolina is a state in the southeastern United States of America. It is on the Atlantic coast. The land near the coast is low. In the center of the state are rolling hills and woodland. To the west are mountains. The weather is warmer nearer the coast and cooler in the mountains.

A couple explore Merchant's Mill Pond State Park in a canoe.

In the past

Long ago, the Cherokee people lived in villages in North Carolina. They farmed, hunted, and fished. Other groups lived along the coast.

Life in North Carolina

In North Carolina, farmers raise hogs, turkeys, and chickens. The main crop is tobacco. Factories in the state process the tobacco and other farm products. Factory workers in North Carolina also produce more furniture and textiles than in any other state. Along the coast, fishermen and women bring in crabs, shrimp, clams, and fish.

DID YOU KNOW?

The first successful powered airplane flight took place near Kitty Hawk, North Carolina. It was made in 1903 by brothers Orville and Wilbur Wright.

North Carolina

FACT FILE

BECAME A STATE...	1789 (12th state)
LAND AREA.........	48,711 square miles (29th largest land area)
POPULATION	8,407,248 (11th largest population)
OTHER NAMES	Tar Heel State, Old North State
CAPITAL CITY	Raleigh

North Dakota

see also: United States of America

North Dakota is a state in the northern United States of America. It is on the northern Great Plains. The land is mostly flat grassland and low hills. Winters in North Dakota are long and cold. There is very little rain in summer or winter.

In the past

Dakota is the name of a Native American tribe that lived in North Dakota long ago. The Dakota were Sioux Indians. Different groups of Sioux and other Plains Indians lived and hunted on the Great Plains before white settlers came in the 1800s and 1900s to start farming.

DID YOU KNOW?

The International Peace Garden is on the border of North Dakota and Canada. It is dedicated to world peace.

These are the rolling hills of Theodore Roosevelt National Park, North Dakota.

Life in North Dakota

Today, farmland covers about 90 percent of North Dakota. Wheat is the main crop. Farmers also raise sunflowers, barley, rye, and cattle. The state produces a lot of coal and oil, too. Visitors come to North Dakota to hunt wild birds and to fish.

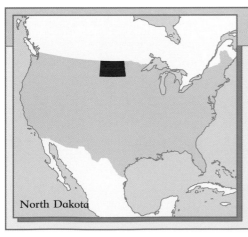

North Dakota

FACT FILE

BECAME A STATE... 1889 (39th state)

LAND AREA......... 68,976 square miles
(17th largest land area)

POPULATION 633,837
(48th most populated state)

OTHER NAME ...... Peace Garden State

CAPITAL CITY ...... Bismarck

North Korea

see also: Asia, South Korea

North Korea is a country in Asia. It is on the Pacific coast. There are hills and mountains over most of the land. North Korea is usually cold in winter. Summer is hot and wet. Three-fourths of the land is covered in forests.

Living in North Korea

Nearly half of the people work on farms or they fish. The main crops are rice, vegetables, and fruit. Farm machinery, chemicals, and cement are made in factories.

Some North Koreans follow the teachings of Confucius. He was an ancient Chinese thinker. He taught that everyone should respect people who are older than they are.

People wear colorful costumes on special days. They do dances from the past.

All school children belong to the group called the Young Pioneers. Young Pioneers learn about their country's communist government.

DID YOU KNOW?

The country of Korea was divided into two countries in 1945. The countries are North Korea and South Korea.

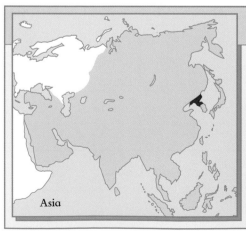

Asia

FACT FILE

PEOPLE	North Koreans
POPULATION	about 23 million
MAIN LANGUAGE	Korean
CAPITAL CITY	Pyongyang
MONEY	North Korean won
HIGHEST MOUNTAIN	Mount Paektu—9,006 feet
LONGEST RIVER	Yalu River—490 miles

Northern Ireland

see also: Europe, United Kingdom

Northern Ireland is part of the United Kingdom. Northern Ireland is on the island of Ireland. It has hills with mountains. The mountains drop steeply to the sea. The climate is mild and wet.

There are many ancient castles in Northern Ireland. This is Carrickfergus Castle on the coast.

Living in Northern Ireland

There is plenty of good grass to raise dairy cows. Some farmers grow flax. Flax is a crop used to make linen cloth. Many factories make electrical goods and parts for aircraft and ships.

Northern Ireland has had violence for more than 30 years. The fighting is about who should govern the country. Many groups are working for peace.

DID YOU KNOW?

The Giant's Causeway is stones that look like steps. The steps reach out into the sea. Legends say that the steps were built by a giant. The stones were really formed by a flow of hot rock. The rock cooled into oddly-shaped columns.

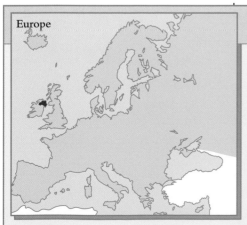

Europe

FACT FILE

PEOPLE	British, Irish
POPULATION	almost 2 million
MAIN LANGUAGE	English
CAPITAL CITY	Belfast
MONEY	Pound sterling
HIGHEST MOUNTAIN	Slieve Donard–2,796 feet
LONGEST RIVER	River Bann–76 miles

Norway

see also: Arctic, Europe, Vikings

Norway is a country in northwest Europe. There are mountains and high flatlands. The coast has long, narrow bays. These bays are called *fjords*. Winters are cold. Summers are hot. The weather is warmer on the coast.

Living in Norway

Most Norwegians live in cities and towns. There is gas and oil in the rocks under the North Sea. The gas and oil are brought to shore in special pipes and then sold to other countries.

The people catch and eat fish called herring. Herring is served in many ways. Lingonberries grow during the short summers. The berries are made into jam. Long ago, Norway was part of the Viking kingdom. Viking designs are still used in crafts, cloth, and metalwork.

These brightly painted houses are in the town of Bergen. They were built for merchants 500 years ago.

DID YOU KNOW?

Bronze Age rock carvings in Norway show the world's first skiers. The carvings are over 4,000 years old.

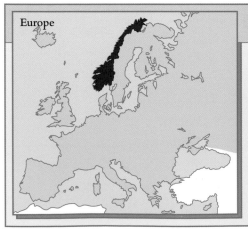

Europe

FACT FILE

PEOPLE	Norwegians
POPULATION	about 4 million
MAIN LANGUAGE	Norwegian
CAPITAL CITY	Oslo
MONEY	Krone
HIGHEST MOUNTAIN	Galdhøpiggen—8,103 feet
LONGEST RIVER	Glåmma—379 miles

Number

see also: Computer, Money

People use numbers to count things. They use numbers to tell how many of something. The special symbols called numerals are used to write numbers. People who study numbers are called mathematicians.

The first numbers

One of the earliest ways of counting was called decimal. Decimal is what most people use today. Decimal is based on the number ten. Ten was chosen because it is easy to count on your fingers. Two sets of fingers and two thumbs make ten.

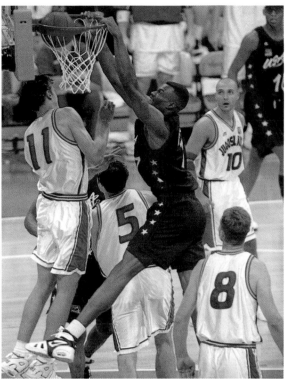

The big numbers on these basketball players' shirts help to identify the players.

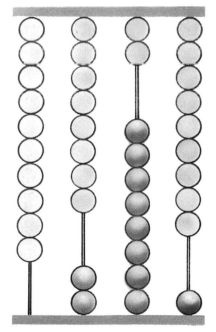

The abacus is an old Chinese counting machine. It is still used in some countries. This abacus is showing the number 281.

Why are numbers important?

Everyone needs numbers. Numbers are used to count things. Numbers are used to count how many people can be safely allowed into a football game. Numbers tell the score of the game. Stores use numbers to count the things they have to sell and to tell how many things they need to order. They use numbers to tell customers how much they owe.

DID YOU KNOW?

Computers do not use decimal numbers. All the information in a computer uses patterns of 0s and 1s. This system is called binary. Binary is based on the number two. In binary, the number two is written 10.

Nutrition

see also: Food Chain, Human Body

Nutrition is the food that humans and animals eat to stay alive. Food is needed as fuel. The fuel keeps the body running. Fuel gives the body the energy it needs. The body uses the important parts in food. These food parts are called nutrients.

DID YOU KNOW?

The energy in food is measured in calories. The more active a person is, the more calories his or her body needs for energy.

Healthful eating

A balanced diet has all the foods a body needs. A balanced diet means eating the right amounts of the different nutrients. A person can become ill if he or she does not have a balanced diet. Millions of people die each year of starvation.

They starve because they don't get enough to eat. Other people become ill or die from malnutrition. The word malnutrition means "bad nutrition." Malnutrition happens when people eat the wrong foods.

MyPyramid
STEPS TO A HEALTHIER YOU
MyPyramid.gov

GRAINS   VEGETABLES   FRUITS   MILK   MEAT & BEANS

Make half your grains whole
Eat some whole-meal grain cereals, breads, crackers, rice or pasta every day for energy.

Vary your veggies
A variety of vegetables give minerals that the body needs.

Focus on fruits
These give important vitamins and fiber.

Get your calcium-rich foods
This provides calcium for healthy bones and teeth.

Go lean with protein
These give protein to help children grow.

Ocean

see also: Water

An ocean is a very big area of water. There are four oceans: the Atlantic, the Arctic, the Indian, and the Pacific. Oceans are much bigger than seas. The Pacific Ocean is the biggest ocean. The Arctic Ocean is the smallest. About three-fourths of the earth's surface is covered by water.

> ### DID YOU KNOW?
> The deepest part in all of the oceans is in the Mariana Trench in the Pacific Ocean. It is nearly seven miles deep.

Under the water

The bottom of the ocean is called the ocean bed. Some of the ocean bed is flat. The deepest parts of the oceans are called trenches. There are also underwater mountain ranges. Some islands are really the tops of underwater mountains. Some of the underwater mountains are active volcanoes. Water flows in the oceans in patterns called currents. The Gulf Stream is a warm current. It flows across the Atlantic Ocean.

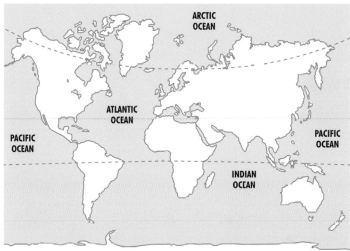

the oceans of the world

People and oceans

Ships carry goods across the oceans. People fish in the oceans. They also enjoy sailing and other water sports. People dump waste in the oceans. This causes pollution. Oil spills are pollution, too. Seabirds, fish, and other animals can die when an ocean gets polluted.

Icebergs are large masses of ice that break off glaciers in the Arctic and in Antarctica. Icebergs float in the oceans.

Octopus

see also: Mollusk, Squid

The octopus is a large mollusk. It has eight legs called tentacles. The octopus has no bones and no shell. It lives on the sea floor. The octopus protects itself by spraying a fluid called ink at its enemies. The common octopus is found in all warm oceans. The giant octopus is found in the Pacific Ocean.

Octopus families

Each octopus makes its own nest in gravel or in the rocks. This nest is called a lair. The female lays many thousands of eggs inside her lair. She moves water over her eggs. This keeps the eggs clean for months until they hatch. She never goes out to hunt.

OCTOPUS FACTS

NUMBER OF KINDS	about 50
COLOR	many different colors
LENGTH	up to 11 feet with tentacles (23 feet across)
WEIGHT	up to 154 lbs.
STATUS	common
LIFE SPAN	2 to 3 years
ENEMIES	people

skin that changes color to help the octopus hide

suckers for holding onto rocks and food

siphon pushes water out very fast to help the octopus move

a deep-sea octopus

These baby Australian octopuses are just hatching.

MEAT EATER

An octopus eats crabs, lobsters, and small shellfish. It uses its powerful beak to crush the shells.

Ohio

see also: United States of America

Ohio is a state in the eastern United States of America. Much of the land is flat with rolling hills. In the north, Ohio borders Lake Erie, one of the Great Lakes. Most of the state has good, rich soil for farming. Ohio has mild weather and gets plenty of rain.

A country lane cuts through farmland in rural Ohio.

Life in Ohio

Today, most people in Ohio live in cities. Ohio has several large cities even though it is not a very large state. Cleveland and Toledo on Lake Erie are busy ports.

Manufacturing, transportation, and trading goods are important industries in Ohio. Goods that are made and traded include steel, metal products, and rubber products.

DID YOU KNOW?

Long ago, the Hopewell people in Ohio built huge mounds out of dirt. Many of the mounds are near Chillicothe, Ohio. Looking down from above, some mounds are shaped like giant animals.

Food is another important industry. Farmers raise corn, fruit, vegetables, and hogs. Even more people process food in Ohio's factories. They bake bread, pack meat, and make cheese.

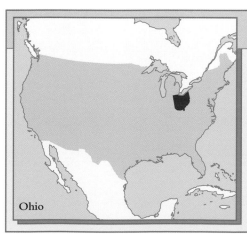

Ohio

FACT FILE

BECAME A STATE	1803 (17th state)
LAND AREA	40,948 square miles (35th largest land area)
POPULATION	11,435,798 (7th most populated state)
OTHER NAME	Buckeye State
CAPITAL CITY	Columbus

Oklahoma

see also: United States of America

Oklahoma is a state in the southern United States of America. In the east, there are hills and small mountains. The center and west of the state are on the plains. The state is dry in the western part and more humid in the east. The weather in Oklahoma is mostly warm. Sometimes there are tornadoes.

Life in Oklahoma

Most people in Oklahoma live in cities. Oklahoma's two largest cities are Oklahoma City and Tulsa. They were built near oil and gas fields. Oil and gas production is an important industry in Oklahoma. Many people also work in factories. They make machinery and transportation equipment.

Oklahoma City is the state's capital.

DID YOU KNOW?

The land that is now Oklahoma was once part of Indian Territory. Many Native Americans came to Indian Territory along the Trail of Tears in the 1830s. They were the Cherokee, Choctaw, Chickasaw, Creek, and Seminole people. They had lost their homes farther east.

Outside of the cities, farmland covers a lot of the state. Farmers raise wheat, sorghum, hay, cattle, hogs, and chickens.

Oklahoma

FACT FILE

	OKLAHOMA

BECAME A STATE... 1907 (46th state)

LAND AREA......... 68,667 square miles
(19th largest land area)

POPULATION 3,511,532
(28th most populated state)

OTHER NAME ...... Sooner State

CAPITAL CITY ...... Oklahoma City

Olympic Games

see also: Greece, Ancient

The Olympic Games is a sporting competition. People from countries all over the world come to the Olympic Games to compete. The games are held every four years.

The first Olympics

The first Olympics were held in ancient Greece. The games were part of a big religious ceremony. People from all over Greece came. Sporting events were held after the religious ceremonies. There were races, wrestling, boxing, and throwing. The men who won got a crown of laurel leaves.

KEY DATES

776 B.C.	The first Olympics are held in ancient Greece.
A.D. 393	The Roman Emperor, Theodosius I, stops all non-Christian ceremonies, including the Olympics.
1896	The first modern Olympics are held in Athens.
1916	The Olympics are canceled because of World War I.
1940, 1944	The Olympics are canceled because of World War II.

The modern Olympics

The first modern Olympics were held in 1896 in Athens, Greece. It was not a religious ceremony. It was a sporting competition. The modern Olympics include sports such as rifle shooting, as well as races and throwing. Men and women compete. The winner of each event gets a gold medal.

DID YOU KNOW?

Summer Olympics are held every four years. Winter Olympics are also held every four years. There are only two years between Summer and Winter Olympics. This means there are Olympic Games every two years.

Greek vases had pictures of the ancient Olympic sports.

Opera

see also: Drama, Music, Theater

Opera uses singing, acting, and music to tell a story. Usually, the characters in an opera sing their parts of the story. Some operas tell sad stories. Other operas tell funny stories. The music for an opera is played by an orchestra.

This scene is from a famous opera by the German composer Richard Wagner.

European operas

The first operas were written in Italy 400 years ago. Operas spread through Europe. They became very popular.

Many famous composers of classical music wrote operas. Mozart and Wagner wrote operas. Short operas in the 1800s had more spoken words. These are called operettas. The English composers Gilbert and Sullivan wrote many operettas.

Chinese opera

There has been a type of opera in China for many hundreds of years. The stories are usually about adventure or love. There is not much scenery. The costumes and makeup worn by the actors are fancy and detailed.

This shows a scene from a Chinese opera. The only scenery is a painted backdrop.

DID YOU KNOW?

Modern musicals such as *Phantom of the Opera* and *West Side Story* are a kind of operetta.

Opossum

see also: Mammal, Marsupial

The opossum is a mammal. It lives in North America and South America. It is a marsupial. This means the female carries her babies in a pouch. The opossum is related to the marsupial possum of Australia and New Zealand.

OPOSSUM FACTS

NUMBER OF KINDS	77
COLOR	black, gray, brown, or white
LENGTH	41 inches
WEIGHT	up to 13 lbs.
STATUS	common
LIFE SPAN	about 2 years
ENEMIES	people

Opossum families

Each adult opossum lives in a nest. The nest is made of dead leaves. The nest can be in a hollow tree, under a pile of dead wood, or in an old burrow. A female opossum can have 25 babies at a time. She can only feed twelve or thirteen of them. The others die. The live babies stay in the pouch for ten weeks. They come out to live in the nest when they are too big for the pouch.

an opossum

very good ears for listening for prey at night

long, curly tail for holding onto branches

strong claws for climbing and digging

A female opossum can carry her young on her back when she goes out to hunt.

PLANT AND MEAT EATER

Some opossums eat fruit and berries. The Virginia opossum of North America eats mostly rodents. It will also kill hens.

Orchestra

see also: Classical Music, Musical Instrument

An orchestra is a large group of musicians. They play together. The most common kind of orchestra has stringed, woodwind, brass, and percussion instruments. It plays classical music. It also plays other music written for these instruments.

DID YOU KNOW?

The conductor faces the orchestra. He or she moves his or her hands in the air. The conductor is guiding the orchestra through the music. He or she reminds the different musicians when to play. The conductor helps to keep the speed and rhythm correct.

The first orchestra

Claudio Monteverdi was a composer. He lived in Italy 400 years ago. He was the first to write music for an orchestra. Since then, new instruments have been invented. Orchestras have changed.

Other groups of musicians play different instruments together. Gamelan orchestras in Indonesia play mainly percussion instruments. *Balalaika* orchestras in Russia play different sizes of the stringed instrument called *balalaika.*

Orchestras today

Today composers still write for the classical orchestra. Some composers add unusual sounds for the orchestra to play. The sounds might be car horns and alarm clocks.

Some composers use a computer or an electronic keyboard. This can copy the different sounds of instruments in an orchestra. The composer can create the sound of a full orchestra without a real orchestra.

This is how a classical orchestra is usually seated for a concert.

Oregon

see also: United States of America

Oregon is a state in the northwestern United States of America. It is on the Pacific coast. Much of the state is covered in mountains and forests. There are wide valleys and deep canyons, too. The weather is mild and rainy along the coast. The eastern region is dry and can be cold in winter.

Life in Oregon

Many people earn their living from the state's land and waters. They cut logs and make wood products. Factory workers make paper products. Other people catch salmon along the coast and in the Columbia River. Farmland in western valleys is good for growing fruit. Farmers in the eastern part of the state grow wheat and raise cattle.

A kayak floats across Lost Lake, with Mount Hood in the background.

DID YOU KNOW?

Crater Lake in Oregon is the deepest lake in the United States. It plunges nearly 2,000 feet at its deepest point.

The lumber and fishing industries in Oregon are controlled. People want to make sure natural resources don't run out. Newer industries in Oregon are replacing lumber and fishing jobs. Many people work in factories making electronic products.

FACT FILE

Oregon

STATE OF OREGON
1859

BECAME A STATE	1859 (33rd state)
LAND AREA	95,997 square miles (10th largest land area)
POPULATION	3,559,596 (27th most populated state)
OTHER NAME	Beaver State
CAPITAL CITY	Salem

Ostrich

see also: Bird

The ostrich is the largest bird in the world. It lives in the grasslands of central and southern Africa. The ostrich cannot fly. It can run at 37 miles per hour. This is faster than all other African animals except the cheetah. The ostrich's eggs are the biggest eggs of any living creature. A male ostrich's kick is so powerful that it can injure a lion.

Ostrich families

A female ostrich is called a hen. A male ostrich makes several nests in the soil. The nests are called scrapes. The male's favorite female chooses one scrape. She lays her eggs in it. Other females lay eggs in the same nest. Chicks from several nests form a large flock. The flock is guarded by only one or two adults.

OSTRICH FACTS

NUMBER OF KINDS	1
COLOR	black/brown, white, and pink
HEIGHT	up to 9 feet
WEIGHT	up to 330 lbs.
STATUS	some endangered
LIFE SPAN	up to 40 years
ENEMIES	hyenas, jackals, people

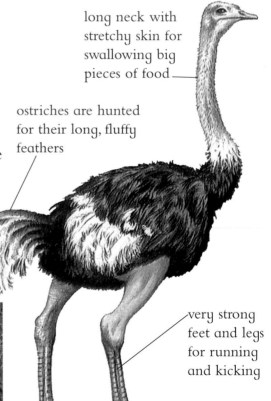

long neck with stretchy skin for swallowing big pieces of food

ostriches are hunted for their long, fluffy feathers

very strong feet and legs for running and kicking

an ostrich

PLANT AND INSECT EATER

An ostrich eats plants, shoots, leaves, flowers, seeds, and insects. It also swallows grit and small stones. This helps it digest its food.

An adult ostrich watches over the eggs. Only the male and his favorite hen look after the eggs.

Otter

see also: Mammal

The otter is a playful mammal. It spends most of its time in water. Most kinds of otters live in rivers. The sea otter lives in the Pacific Ocean.

Otter families

A male otter is called a dog. A baby otter is called a cub. A river otter's home is a burrow called a holt. Each dog otter has two or more females in his large territory. Each female feeds and teaches her own two or three cubs.

Male and female sea otters live in separate groups for most of the year. Female sea otters only have one cub at a time. The sea otter doesn't have a home. It ties itself to a piece of seaweed before going to sleep.

OTTER FACTS

NUMBER OF KINDS	6
COLOR	brown
LENGTH	up to 4 feet
WEIGHT	up to 100 lbs.
STATUS	some threatened
LIFE SPAN	up to 20 years
ENEMIES	people

oily, waterproof fur for keeping dry and warm

strong jaws and sharp teeth for catching fish

strong tail for steering while swimming and fighting

webbed feet for swimming

an Asian short-clawed otter

This female sea otter is floating on her back. Her baby sleeps on her stomach.

MEAT AND INSECT EATER

A river otter eats mostly fish. It eats eels. Otters also eat frogs, crayfish, and water insects. The sea otter eats abalone. This is a kind of shellfish.

Owl

see also: Bird

The owl is a bird of prey. It hunts at night. There are many different kinds of owls. They live all over the world.

Owl families

The male and female owl make a nest in a tree or a farm building. The female owl lays one egg every few days. She may lay as many as seven eggs. The female sits on the eggs. The male brings her food.

A baby owl is called an owlet. When the owlets are a few days old, the female leaves the nest to hunt for food. The owlets leave home after a few weeks.

OWL FACTS

NUMBER OF KINDS	133
COLOR	usually brown or brown and white
LENGTH	up to 28 inches
WEIGHT	up to 4 pounds
STATUS	common
LIFE SPAN	up to 18 years
ENEMIES	eagles, buzzards, people

large and powerful eyes to see in the dark

soft feathers for making less noise when flying

small, sharp bill for ripping meat

a barn owl

strong claws and feet for holding food and fighting

A female great horned owl looks after her owlets in a nest in a tree.

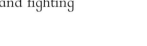

MEAT EATER

An owl catches mice, rats, and voles. The owl drops down from the sky and grabs them in its strong claws. Owls that eat fish have no feathers on their legs.

Oxygen

see also: Air, Lung, Plant

Oxygen is one of the gases in the air. It is the part of the air that our bodies use. Humans and animals die without oxygen.

Plants and oxygen

About one-fifth of fresh air is oxygen. All humans and animals use oxygen when they breathe. Then they breathe out a gas called carbon dioxide. Plants take carbon dioxide from the air. The plants give out oxygen. If there were no plants, oxygen would get used up.

Using oxygen

Fires burn only when they have oxygen. One way to put out a fire is to make sure there is no oxygen. Covering a fire with foam or a special fire-blanket takes away the oxygen.

Oxygen also helps metals to corrode. Metals won't corrode if the oxygen is kept away. Covering metals with paint stops the corroding. Paint keeps the oxygen out.

Pure oxygen can make fire burn very strongly. This is a welding torch. Oxygen makes a flame that is hot enough to melt metal.

Human beings cannot take oxygen out of water like fish can. This diver has a tank of oxygen. He breathes in oxygen through a mouthpiece.

DID YOU KNOW?

If oxygen is cooled down it will turn into a liquid. Rocket engines use liquid oxygen to burn their fuel.

Painting

see also: Art

Painters make marks on a surface. They use paints such as oil paints or watercolors. The surface can be paper, wood, canvas, plaster, stone, or even a person.

The first painting

Painting is one of the oldest kinds of art. The earliest paintings were made by prehistoric people on cave walls. Many cave paintings are about hunting. They were probably painted to bring good luck to the hunters. The paintings might also tell of a successful hunt.

Painting became important over many, many years. Powerful people asked artists to paint pictures of them, their families, or the things they owned. Painters also made religious paintings. Some painters painted pictures of the local scenery.

The tribespeople of Papua New Guinea paint their bodies.

LEONARDO DA VINCI (1452–1519)

Leonardo da Vinci was born in Italy. He was a painter, sculptor, architect, engineer, and scientist. His famous portrait called *Mona Lisa* (above) is one of the most popular paintings in the world. Another of his famous paintings is *The Last Supper*. It is a large picture of Jesus and the Apostles. Da Vinci painted it onto the wall of an Italian monastery.

DID YOU KNOW?

Some paintings made in the last 100 years are not pictures of people, places, and things. Instead, the painters try to show ideas or feelings. They use colors, patterns, and shapes. This is called abstract painting.

Pakistan

see also: Asia

Pakistan is a country in the south of Asia. There are high mountains over half the country. The Indus River flows through the lowlands. The weather is hot and wet in summer. It is warm and dry in winter.

DID YOU KNOW?

Pakistan became an independent country in 1947, at the same time as India.

Living in Pakistan

Farmers grow rice, wheat, and vegetables. They cut flat fields into the steep hillsides. This makes more land for farming. Factories in the cities make clothes, rugs, and food products.

Most Pakistanis follow the religion of Islam. They celebrate Islamic festivals. A favorite food is rice with hot curries.

This fabric shop sells colorful and decorated cloth. It can be used to make clothing. The most expensive cloth is silk with threads of real gold.

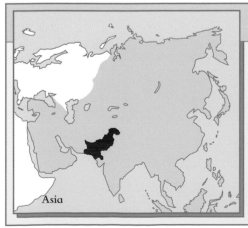

Asia

FACT FILE

PEOPLE	Pakistanis
POPULATION	about 159 million
MAIN LANGUAGE	Urdu
CAPITAL CITY	Islamabad
BIGGEST CITY	Karachi
MONEY	Rupee
HIGHEST MOUNTAIN	K2 (Godwin Austen)—28,261 ft.
LONGEST RIVER	Indus River—1,925 miles

Panama

see also: North America, Waterway

Panama is a small country in Central America. It is on a narrow strip of land. The Atlantic Ocean is on one side. The Pacific Ocean is on the other side. There are mountains over most of the country. The weather is mostly hot and rainy. Rain forests cover about half of Panama.

Living in Panama

Most people work in factories. They also work with the ships that pass through the Panama Canal. About one-third of the people are farmers. Farmers grow rice, corn, beans, bananas, and coffee.

Panamanians celebrate Christian festivals, saints' days, and local Native American festivals. In one Native American festival, young men throw light, soft balsa tree logs at each other.

The Panama Canal opened in 1914. Ships sail through the Panama Canal between the Atlantic Ocean and the Pacific Ocean.

DID YOU KNOW?

It takes up to nine hours for a large ship to go through the Panama Canal. Going through the canal cuts 7,452 miles off the old journey. That journey went around the southern tip of South America.

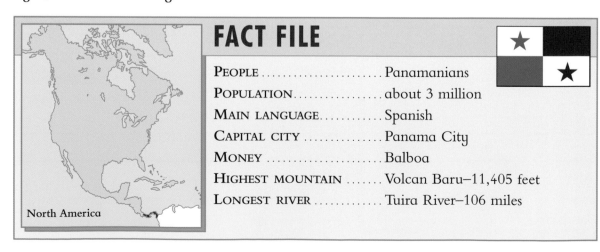

North America

FACT FILE

PEOPLE	Panamanians
POPULATION	about 3 million
MAIN LANGUAGE	Spanish
CAPITAL CITY	Panama City
MONEY	Balboa
HIGHEST MOUNTAIN	Volcan Baru—11,405 feet
LONGEST RIVER	Tuira River—106 miles

Panda

see also: Mammal

A panda is a furry mammal. There are two kinds of panda. The giant panda looks a bit like a black and white bear. The smaller, red panda looks a bit like a chubby cat. There are only about 1,000 giant pandas living wild in China. The rest live in zoos.

PANDA FACTS

NUMBER OF KINDS	2
LENGTH	giant panda: up to 5 feet red panda: up to 2 feet
WEIGHT	giant panda: 230 lbs. red panda: 7 to 11 lbs.
LIFE SPAN	up to 20 years
STATUS	endangered
ENEMIES	people

Panda families

Giant panda babies are called cubs. Cubs only weigh about 4 ounces when they are born. The cubs leave their mothers when they are a year old. Adult giant pandas live most of their lives on their own. They push through the forest, climbing trees and eating.

thumb-type bones on paws for holding bamboo shoots

thick, waterproof fur for keeping warm and dry

a young giant panda

Pandas are endangered because the bamboo that they eat is disappearing.

PLANT EATER

Pandas eat a kind of tall grass called bamboo. Giant pandas have to eat for at least twelve hours a day to stay alive.

Papua New Guinea

see also: Australia and Oceania

Papua New Guinea is a country north of Australia. It includes the eastern half of the island of New Guinea and 600 small islands. Mountains with thick forest are in the center. The climate is hot. It rains a lot.

Living in Papua New Guinea

Most Papuans live in the country. Farmers grow bananas and root crops. They raise pigs. There are gold, copper, and silver mines. Timber, fish, coffee, coconuts, and cocoa are sold to other countries.

Fish and other seafood are served with yams, sweet potatoes, or *taros*. *Taros* is the soft insides of the sago palm. Meat, vegetables, and herbs are baked in an underground oven. The oven is called a *mumu*. Many of the islands are famous for their dances. New Ireland island has 50 different dances.

This house is made of wood. It is built on stilts to keep it dry. It is the home for an entire village.

DID YOU KNOW?

The bird on the Papuan flag is called a kumul. It is a type of bird of paradise.

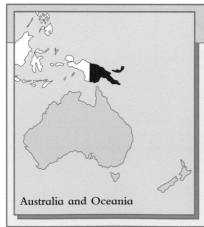

Australia and Oceania

FACT FILE

PEOPLE	Papuans
POPULATION	about 5 million
MAIN LANGUAGES	English, Tok pisin, Motu
CAPITAL CITY	Port Moresby
MONEY	Kina
HIGHEST MOUNTAIN	Mount Wilhelm—14,793 feet
LONGEST RIVER	Sepik River—422 miles

Parrot

see also: Bird

A parrot is a brightly colored bird. It lives in warm countries all around the world. Most parrots live in forests. A few parrots live in the desert.

Parrot families

Parrots live together in large flocks. The female usually makes a nest in a tree. The female lays up to six eggs. She sits on them. The male brings her food. The babies are called chicks. The chicks stay with their parents. They leave when it is time to have chicks of their own.

PLANT EATER

Parrots have specially-shaped big beaks for eating fruit and seeds. Some parrots eat flowers.

PARROT FACTS	
NUMBER OF KINDS	about 320
COLOR	many colors
LENGTH	up to 3 feet
WEIGHT	up to 6 lbs.
STATUS	rare in wild
LIFE SPAN	about 40 years
ENEMIES	eagles, falcons, people

large beak for cracking nuts and seeds, and for holding on when climbing

strong feet for climbing and holding on

long tail to help balance

a scarlet macaw parrot

This Australian ring-necked parrot has just landed by its nest in a tree hollow.

Penguin

see also: Antarctica, Bird

The penguin is a bird. It cannot fly, but it can swim very well. It can stay under water for several minutes. There are eighteen kinds of penguins. Penguins mostly live in and around the cold Antarctic.

Penguin families

Penguins spend months eating at sea. Then they come onto land. The male arrives first. He finds a place to nest and wait for the female. Together they make a nest of rocks. The female lays one egg. The parents take turns looking after the egg. Then they take turns caring for the baby. The baby is called a chick.

Chicks are very fluffy. This keeps them warm. A few adult penguins look after lots of chicks together. A group of penguins is called a rookery.

PENGUIN FACTS

NUMBER OF KINDS........	18
COLOR.......	black and white
HEIGHT......	up to 44 inches
WEIGHT......	up to 88 lbs.
STATUS.......	common
LIFE SPAN....	up to 20 years
ENEMIES......	sea leopards, people

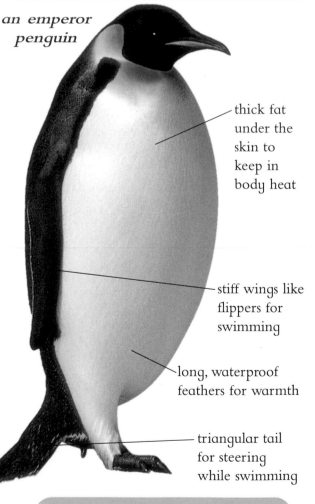

an emperor penguin

thick fat under the skin to keep in body heat

stiff wings like flippers for swimming

long, waterproof feathers for warmth

triangular tail for steering while swimming

Emperor penguin parents take turns. One parent looks after the chick while the other parent goes out to sea to eat.

MEAT EATER

A penguin catches its food under water. It eats krill, crabs, fish, and squid.